For You,
Mother

Over my slumbers
your
loving

ever known; and so very beautiful. . . . Within our home, she was an abundance of love, discipline, fun, affection, strength, tenderness, encouragement, understanding, inspiration, support.

Leontyne Price

Momma was home.
She was the most totally
human being that I had

Lin Yutang

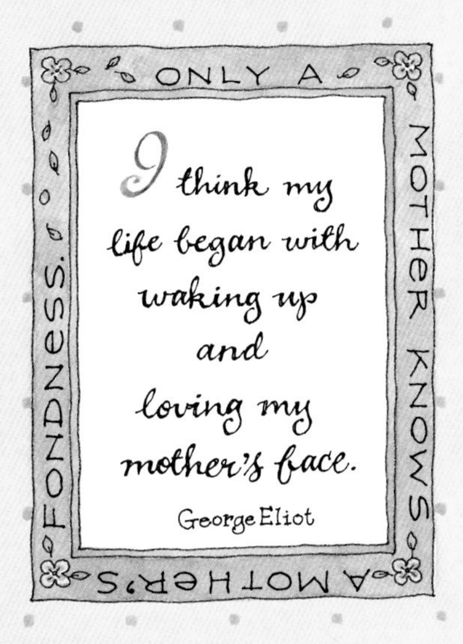

Lady Mary Wortley Montague

as

I never

was

when

I

was not

one.

Margaret Atwood

Because I am a mother, I am capable of being shocked:

A MOTHER

♥ ♥ ♥

HOURS – 24 hours per day
7 days per week
365 days per year

WAGE – $0

DUTIES – Cooking, cleaning, laundry, teacher, chauffeuring, baby-sitting, referee, nurse & so on. . . .

Inquire Within!

The phrase
"working mother"
is
redundant.

Jane Sellman

Anyone who thinks
mother love is as
soft and golden-eyed
as a purring cat
should see a
cat defending
her kittens.

Pam Brown

be to write about a
hurricane in its
perfect power. Or the
climbing, falling colors
of a rainbow.

Maya Angelou

To describe my mother would

Edith F. Hunter

The walks and talks
we have with
our two-year-olds
in red boots
have a great deal
to do with the
values they will
cherish as adults.

My mother is
a poem I'll never be
able to write
though
everything I write
is a poem
to my mother.

Sharon Doubiago

Jewish proverb

Madeleine L'Engle

I looked at this tiny, perfect creature and it was as though a light switch had been turned on. A great rush of love, mother love, flooded out of me.

The hand that rocks the cradle is the hand that rules the world.

W. S. Ross

There never was
a child so lovely
but his mother was
glad to get him
asleep.

Ralph Waldo Emerson

Who ran to help me
when I fell,
And would some
pretty story tell,
Or kiss the place
to make it
well?
My mother.

Ann Taylor

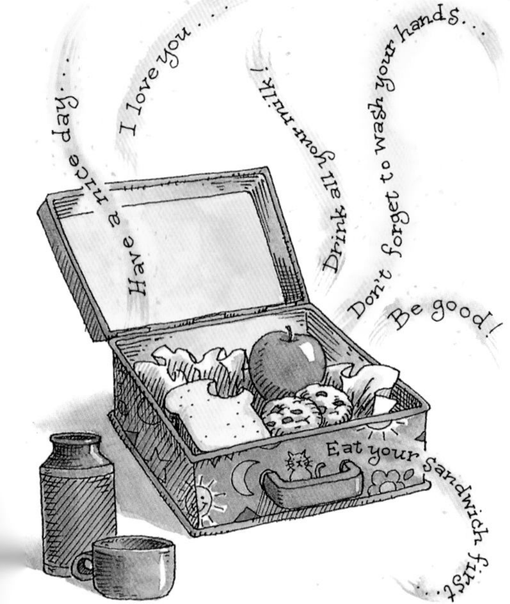

Have a nice day. . .

I love you . . .

Drink all your milk!

Don't forget to wash your hands. . .

Be good!

Eat your sandwich first. . .

In a child's
lunch basket,
a mother's
thoughts.

Don't eat too fast...

Japanese proverb

and strength demands
are made not only
every hour of the day,
but often
every
hour of the
night.

Theodore Roosevelt

No ordinary work
done by a man is
either as hard or as
responsible as
the work of a woman who
is bringing up a
family of small children;
for upon her time

I love her for that.
I love the
fact that she wanted
to give birth
to her own wings.
Erica Jong

My mother wanted
me to be her wings,
to fly as
she never quite had
the courage to do.

Every beetle
is a
gazelle
in the eyes of
its
mother.

Moorish proverb

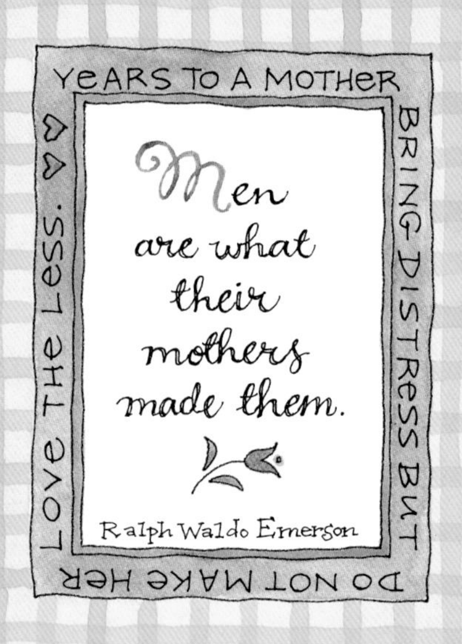

William Wordsworth

...Mothers and housewives are the only workers who do not have regular time off. They are the great vacationless class.

Madeleine L'Engle

and most mothers

together.

Pearl S. Buck

Some are kissing
mothers
and some are
!scolding!! mothers,
but
it is love
just the same,

In search of my mother's garden I found my own.

Alice Walker

Where there is a
mother in the house,
matters speed well.

Amos Bronson Alcott

A MOTHER'S LOVE AND PRAYERS AND TEARS ARE SELDOM LOST ON EVEN THE MOST WAYWARD CHILD.

Most mothers are instinctive philosophers.

Harriet Beecher Stowe

A.E. Davis

My mother made a brilliant impression upon my childhood life. She shone for me like the evening star — I loved her dearly.

Winston Churchill

When a mother
finally decides
to give her daughter
some advice,
the mother
usually learns
plenty.

Evan Esar

Loving a child is a circular business... The more you give, the more you get, the more you get, the more you want to give.

Penelope Leach

Any mother
could perform the
jobs of several
air-traffic
controllers
with ease.

Lisa Alther

My mother's hands
are cool and fair,
they can do anything.
Delicate mercies
hide them there
like flowers in
the spring.

Anna Hempstead
Branch

WHO TAKES THE CHILD BY THE HAND TAKES THE MOTHER BY THE HEART.
DANISH PROVERB

It is you, mother.

Thomas Carlyle

Who is it that loves me and will love me forever with an affection which no chance, no misery, no crime of mine can do away? —

A mother's arms
are made of
tenderness
and
children
sleep
soundly
in
them.

Victor Hugo

Charles Lamb

but at least we
would get off
the ground.

Zora Neale Hurston

All

that I am or hope to be
I owe to my

angel mother.

Abraham Lincoln

Children
are the
anchors
that
hold a mother
to life.

Sophocles

A mother is a person
who, seeing there are
only four pieces of pie
for five people,

promptly announces she
never did care for pie.

Tenneva Jordan

A mother is not a
person to lean on
but a person to make
leaning unnecessary.

Dorothy Canfield Fisher

A mother understands what a child does not say.

Jewish proverb

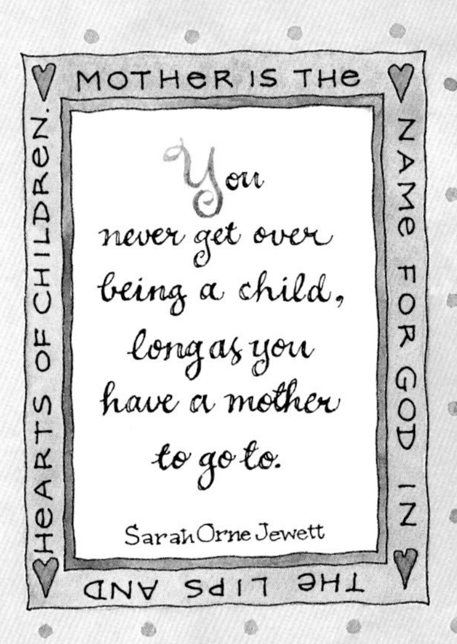

William Makepeace Thackeray

The mother's heart is the child's schoolroom.

Henry Ward Beecher

Mothers...
are the first
book read
and the last
put aside
in every child's
library.

C. Lenox Remond

Before becoming a mother I had a hundred theories on how to bring up children.

Now I have seven children and only one theory: Love them, especially when they least deserve to be loved.

Kate Samperi

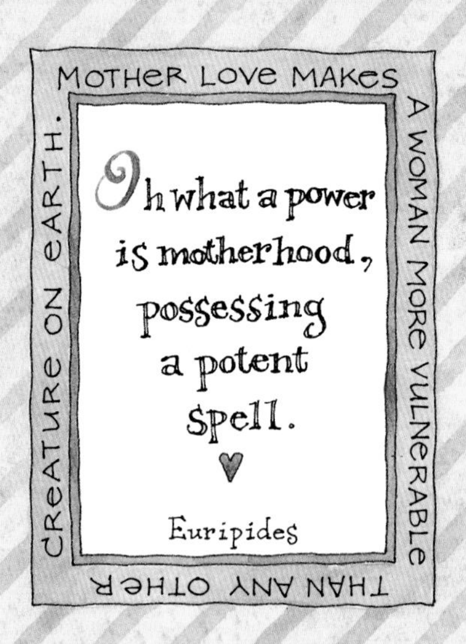
MOTHER LOVE MAKES
A WOMAN MORE VULNERABLE
THAN ANY OTHER
CREATURE ON EARTH.
Oh what a power
is motherhood,
possessing
a potent
spell.
Euripides

Pam Brown

Like one,

like the other.

Like daughter,

like

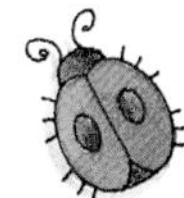

mother.

Anonymous

Mama exhorted her children at every opportunity to "jump at de Sun." We might not land on the sun,

For You, Mother

Ariel Books

Andrews McMeel Publishing

Kansas City

For information write Andrews McMeel Publishing, an Andrews McMeel Universal company, 4520 Main Street, Kansas City, Missouri 64111.

www.andrewsmcmeel.com

ISBN: 0-8362-8171-3
Library of Congress Catalog Card Number: 98-86594

Illustrated by

Robyn Stucki Officer

This book is lovingly
dedicated to her mother ~

Marjorie Curtis Stucki

♥

This book is my way of thanking you for all you've given me— gentle guidance, unconditional love, and constant support. *Thank you, Mom...*

. . . for always be-
lieving in me and
loving me enough to
help me realize my
dreams. Collected
here in this little
volume are words
of gratitude,

devotion, and love
for the woman who
helped me become
who I am today.
It's dedicated to
you,

Mother!

Mother—that was
the bank where
we deposited all
our hurts
and
worries.

T. DeWitt Talmage

The heart of a
mother is a deep abyss
at the bottom of which
you will always
discover
forgiveness.

Honoré de Balzac

A mother's children are like Ideas; none are as wonderful as your own.

Chinese proverb

Youth fades; love droops; the
leaves
of
friendship
fall:
A
mother's
secret love
outlives
them
all.
Oliver Wendell
Holmes

You want to make the most out of every little scrap life gives you. My mother taught me that.

Joyce Maynard

watch keep;
Rock me to
sleep,
mother;
Rock me to
sleep.

Elizabeth Akers Allen

Nobody knows
of the work it makes
To keep the home
together,
Nobody knows of the
steps it takes,
Nobody knows—but
mother.

Anonymous